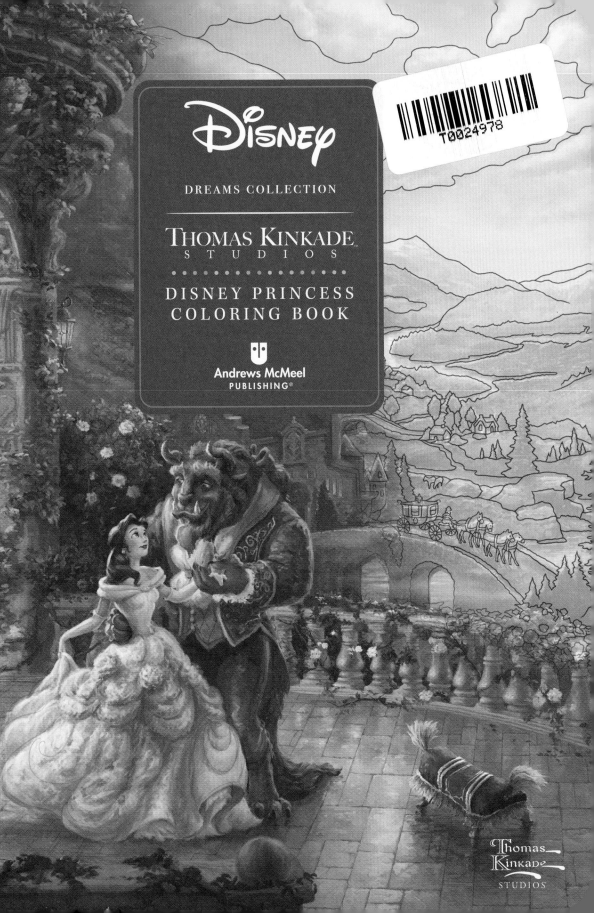

DISNEY

DREAMS COLLECTION

THOMAS KINKADE
S T U D I O S

DISNEY PRINCESS
COLORING BOOK

Andrews McMeel
PUBLISHING®

Jasmine Dancing in the Desert Sunset

Beauty and the Beast II

Mulan Blossoms of Love

The Little Mermaid

Beauty and the Beast II

Snow White and the Seven Dwarfs

Tangled Up In Love

Little Mermaid Falling in Love

The Princess and the Frog

Beauty and the Beast's Winter Enchantment

Snow White Discovers the Cottage

Sleeping Beauty

The Little Mermaid II

Aladdin

Cinderella Wishes Upon a Dream

Snow White Dancing in the Sunlight

Sleeping Beauty Dancing in the Enchanted Light

Pocahontas

Sleeping Beauty

Beauty and the Beast Falling in Love

The Little Mermaid

Jasmine Dancing in the Desert Sunset

Cinderella Dancing in the Starlight

Beauty and the Beast Dancing in the Moonlight

Snow White Dancing in the Sunlight

Mulan Blossoms of Love

Sleeping Beauty Dancing in the Enchanted Light

The Little Mermaid

Beauty and the Beast Falling in Love

Tangled

The Princess and the Frog

Aladdin

Snow White Discovers the Cottage

Tangled Up In Love

Cinderella Dancing in the Starlight

Beauty and the Beast Dancing in the Moonlight

Little Mermaid Falling in Love

Beauty and the Beast Dancing in the Moonlight

Sleeping Beauty

Snow White and the Seven Dwarfs

The Little Mermaid II

Pocahontas

Beauty and the Beast's Winter Enchantment

Tangled

Snow White Dancing in the Sunlight

Cinderella Wishes Upon a Dream

The Little Mermaid II